MW01289958

Faith in Training: A 40 Day Devotional

Pauline Creeden

Published by AltWit Press, 2017.

Faith in Training

Devotional for Horse Lovers

Copyright © 2017 by Pauline Creeden

Cover Design by Cassie Roop of Pink Ink Designs

Edited by Sheila Hollinghead

For Sunday Devotionals, Bible Studies and Giveaways,

Consider subscribing to my newsletter:

http://fatfreefaith.blogspot.com/p/subscribe.html

Introduction:

═══

For those of us who are lucky enough to have them, horses enrich our lives. They each have individual personalities, and we work hard to develop intimate relationships with them. People are often mistaken in feeling that horses are like big dogs. They are nothing like dogs. In fact, they are often more complex than the pets we are used to but so much simpler than the people in our lives.

God wants us to learn from every situation and every relationship. Even the relationship we have with our pets should teach us about Him and His nature. This short 40-day collection of two-minute devotionals is designed to help the reader see God in even the smallest details of life.

Day 1

————

Have I not commanded you? Be strong and of good courage; do not be afraid, nor be dismayed, for the Lord your God is with you wherever you go. (Joshua 1:9)

Horses have a strong flight instinct. Because they are low on the food chain, they know they are one false move away from being someone's dinner. They do not know that lions, tigers, and bears are a rare occurrence and pose little threat to them in the riding arena. It is the job of the handler to develop a trusting relationship with their horse and then face the horse's fears with him. Through time and patience, the handler instills trust and helps the horse become less fearful.

In order to face our fears, we also have to trust the One who is leading us through them. We have to realize that God does not lead us through our fears because He hates us or wants us to fail. God knows that it's only by facing those fears that we can overcome them. And we can only overcome them by relying on our established trust and relationship with God. It is through repeated success in overcoming that we learn to rely on God more, trust him more, and fear circumstances less.

Day 2

The sheep hear his voice; and he calls his own sheep by name and leads them out. And when he brings out his own sheep, he goes before them; and the sheep follow him, for they know his voice. Yet they will by no means follow a stranger, but will flee from him, for they do not know the voice of strangers. (John 10:3-5)

When a horse comes to know and trust his trainer, he will respond immediately to her voice. By nature, horses have a natural herd instinct and will follow the trainer because she has established herself as a trustworthy leader. And the horse also knows that the trainer usually calls him to provide something: food, water, grooming, shelter from the storm, or instruction. Conversely, if a stranger calls the horse, he may look in the direction of the voice out of curiosity, but generally, horses tend to be wary of people they do not know, particularly if they have had bad experiences.

In the same way, our own bad experiences can help us determine whose voice is our Master's and whose voice belongs to a stranger. It is only by developing a relationship with our God that we can know His voice, and know He calls when He wants to provide us with something, even if it's instruction. God is a trustworthy trainer who has our best in mind, whereas a stranger does not and is not worth listening to. From the start, we should work to know whose voice is whose.

Day 3

―――

*T*he leech has two daughters—Give and Give! There are three things that are never satisfied, Four never say, "Enough!": the grave, the barren womb, the earth that is not satisfied with water—and the fire never says "Enough!" (Proverbs 30:15-16)

By nature, horses are grazers. This means they eat virtually all day and all night. They almost never stop eating—except for times of play, work, sleep, or migration. They are not made with a mechanism in their brains which tells them when they are full or when they've eaten too much. In captivity, horses are fed on their human's schedule. Much of what we make for horses is full of seeds and grains which are higher in carbs and fats than their natural grass diet. Additionally, a horse gets only so much grass with each bite and chews grass for long periods of time. On the other hand, grain doesn't necessarily have to be chewed, and it's possible for the horse to eat more than his stomach can tolerate. There are stories of horses with ruptured stomachs who continue to eat, up until the very moment of death.

We are like this also. Our choice of "food" is constant stimulation. We can be occupied with social media, television, games, and electronics all day long. And with each of these gadgets comes the temptation to allow them to overcome our lives. Our time reading the Bible or praying or fellowshipping with God is cut off. We don't want to allow anything to overwhelm us so that we forget what is truly important. Remember when it's time to say, "Enough."

Day 4

He knows the way I have taken; when He has tested me, I will emerge as pure gold. (Job 23:10)

Because of their heightened flight instinct, horses struggle with fear from the day they are born. They are prey animals, and they know it. Everything is out to get them. But through diligent training and handling, their fear can be transformed into trust. The more situations they survive with their trusted handler, the more they trust him. They realize that they are not alone and things become less scary for them. They believe that their handler will get them past the scary time to a place of safety again.

Life is a struggle. In our lives, pain, darkness, and fear are as constant as the rising and setting of the sun or the cycling of the moon. But if we learn God is a reliable source of strength in the times we need him most and we are not alone in our struggles, we are reminded that all of these times are temporary. He knows what we are going through, and He is with us. Placing our trust in Him to carry us through to the other side is all we need to find peace and safety again.

Day 5

―――――

Do you not know? Have you not heard? The Lord is the everlasting God, the Creator of the ends of the earth. He will not grow tired or weary... (Isaiah 40:28)

Often the horse will engage his handler in a battle of wills. Sometimes this resistance can be due to fear or pain, but often, it is due to stubbornness or lack of understanding. The horse does not respond well to excessive punishment and will not bend often to the force of his handler's will. But a patient, consistent handler, will know how much pressure to apply and exactly when to relieve pressure at the slightest bending of the horse in the direction the handler wishes to go. This handler will not tire in the fight to guide the horse in a manner that is preferable to both horse and handler, thereby developing trust as the horse discovers how to understand his handler's will.

Likewise, we find ourselves in a battle of wills with our God, at times almost daily. We resist His direction and get stubborn—dig in our heels and refuse to go in the direction that He wants us to go. Sometimes, we even demand that if God *really* wants us to move, He'd force us to. But God is patient and does not go for aggressive tactics that make us dig in harder. He guides us with the right amount of force to help us understand until we discover the truth; His way is better to begin with.

Day 6

───

A nd they said to Moses, "Speak to us yourself and we will listen. But do not have God speak to us or we will die." (Exodus 20:19)

Some owners and handlers of horses jump into every newfangled training fad. They listen until a new one comes up, and then they hop into the next camp. They learn lots of techniques and tricks to make their horse learn better, and hopefully perform better than before. But often the continual tricks and techniques leave the horse confused, sometimes in worse condition than originally. Their mistake: instead of taking their time and learning about the psychology of the horse from the horse himself, the handler has sought out someone to teach them a short cut. And when the shortcut doesn't work, they aren't to blame—the fad trainer is.

As Christians, we often do the same thing. We listen to the preacher on Sunday, maybe even Wednesday, too. We'll listen to preaching on the radio, or even read devotionals daily. But if we're not spending time in reading the Bible for ourselves, or praying and talking to God, then we are doing nothing but looking for a shortcut. It's easy to blame what we don't like on a preacher's "misinterpretation" of scripture. We can twist things so that we're not really disobeying God. But if we live in communion with Him through prayer and reading the Bible, we cannot deny the conviction we feel when we sin. There is no shortcut or fad that will deepen our relationship with Him or take the place of prayer and study of His word.

7

Day 7

———

There is one who speaks rashly, like the thrust of a sword, but the tongue of the wise brings healing. (Proverbs 12:18)

Wisdom is created through patient learning and keen observation, by concentration and rational choices—not through emotional outbursts and rash decisions. While working with the horse, every action and decision the handler makes will influence the animal. If we are rash with the horse, he will typically respond in kind: emotional outburst for emotional outburst. His fight or flight instinct is bound to kick in. But when dealt with patiently and rationally, it gives the horse time to consider his options, and when he makes the right decision and is rewarded for it through timely praise, his own sense of wisdom can develop.

Likewise, as the saying goes, "people have a habit of becoming what you encourage them to be, not what you nag them to be." God created us to respond in this way. He is the greatest of all encouragers and will not nag you into any behavior. While He treats us patiently and kindly, we learn to behave more like Him. We learn and gain the wisdom He wants to bestow upon us as we follow His leading.

Day 8

———

For I know the thoughts that I think toward you, says the LORD, thoughts of peace and not of evil, to give you a future and a hope. (Jeremiah 29:11)

Often in the development of the horse's training, the handler must use a form of punishment for bad behavior. Even so, this is always for the horse's best interest. A rogue horse is one which refuses to bend to the will of the handler. This horse is dangerous and can cause great harm to itself, other horses, or the humans that handle him. But rogue horses can often be avoided if the handler is patient enough to earn the horse's trust. This trust is developed when the horse believes, even when being punished, that the handler is being fair and is communicating on a level which allows the horse to understand. And even when the horse is going through tough times, he will trust that the handler will help him through.

Sometimes it feels like God is picking on us. We all go through tough times. Sometimes it's reaping what we've sown, and receiving the just results of our own actions. But other times, the trials we are going through seem unfair, and we can't understand why we're going through them. If we believe that God's thoughts toward us and plans for us are good, then we can trust Him to help us through whatever we're enduring, whether we believe we deserve it or not.

Day 9

―――

A gentle answer turns away wrath, but a harsh word stirs up anger. (Proverbs 15:1)

Horses do not respond well to harsh words or actions. It tends to trigger the fight or flight instinct. Generally, a harshly spoken word invokes panic in a horse, and their next step is to run away from the rough treatment or fight against it. That's not to say that a trainer cannot use a stern word when working with a horse—sometimes a quick shout is necessary to help the horse respect the trainer's personal space or to keep him from repeating a bad behavior. But if those harsh moments aren't tempered with gentle words and praises, the horse will become an unwilling partner whose instincts get in the way of training.

In our home life, we deal with people who might irritate us, get in our personal space, or repeat bad behavior, just as the horse will. But if all we use are harsh words because we want that person's behavior to change, it will trigger the person's fight-or-flight instinct, as well. The person may become grumpy and argumentative or run away—sometimes physically, but also mentally by shutting you out. Tempering those harsh, nagging moments with positive praise will help keep the family member's instincts from getting in the way of your relationship as well!

Day 10

Whoever seeks good finds favor, but evil comes to one who searches for it. (Proverbs 11:27)

When modifying a horse's behavior through training, the handler must keep a positive outlook. Expect the best but prepare for the worst. The handler needs to believe that the horse will do what is expected of them and then act accordingly. If the handler fears the worst, their body language and attitude will communicate more to the horse than their words. If the handler expects a fight, the horse will give them one. Even when something bad happens during a training session, the trainer cannot hold a grudge, or the horse will hold one as well.

Henry Ford said, "Whether you think you can or you think you can't, you're right." A positive outlook on the day will produce better results than a negative one, one hundred percent of the time. Even if something bad happens in the morning, and we don't get off on the right foot, we cannot let it set the tone for the whole day. No matter what happens, we must learn to keep circumstances from determining what kind of day we are having. Instead of letting the circumstances drive us, how about we drive our circumstances?

Day 11

―――

There is one who speaks rashly, like the thrust of a sword, but the tongue of the wise brings healing. (Proverbs 12:18)

Rash behavior and words don't mix well with horses. They hate surprises. A good horse handler learns to keep themselves calm, no matter the situation. Even when the horse's instincts kick in and they panic, the handler's panic will only keep the horse in the heightened state of alert, rather than helping him realize the danger he perceived is not as bad as he imagines. A good horse handler can keep calm and use gentle words to help bring healing to the situation, no matter the circumstances. Wisdom in this situation is keeping emotions from having control and bringing the horse down with rational thoughts, words, and behaviors.

People don't do well with surprises either. Staying rational in every situation, and thinking before speaking helps settle and heal a situation. Sometime people say things they don't really mean. In the heat of the moment, we often make decisions we later regret. We can consider ourselves wise when we take a deep breath and think about the consequences of our actions or the words we're about to say. Thinking before acting or speaking is God-ordained wisdom.

Day 12

And without faith it is impossible to please God, because anyone who comes to him must believe that he exists and that he rewards those who earnestly seek him. (Hebrews 11:6)

The trainer only has complete control of the horse when the horse is surrendered to her. But to give this surrender, the horse must trust her completely. This is faith in the horse world—complete trust and belief the trainer will do what she said she will do. And at the end of the training session, a reward reinforces that faith. Sometimes compensation isn't much more than a break or time off. Other times, the reward is exactly what the horse has desired (typically, food). But regardless, the horse trusts the trainer to not ask more than he is ready to handle. And that leads to a benefit in the end.

The faith a person needs to have in God is similar. If we believe Him and trust Him, we will work harder and surrender our will to Him, knowing He will reward us in some manner. Life is easier for us when we give up our will and take on our Lord's. It's not easier if He spoils us. This world and what we think we desire in it will harm us in the end. An alcoholic who drinks all he wants is killing himself in the end. So is the obese person who eats all she wants. That's how the world harms us. But living in the will of God is a surrendered will—where He is in control, and we look to Him for our reward. We need to trust that He will not give us more than we can handle. And that leads to a benefit for us in the end, even if we can't see it right now.

Day 13

———

You are the salt of the earth. But if the salt loses its saltiness, how can it be made salty again? It is no longer good for anything, except to be thrown out and trampled underfoot. (Matthew 5:13)

Salt is necessary for the body to function properly—it controls water intake as well as the function of muscles and the nervous system. While in captivity, horses are given free-choice access to salt in the form of a block of minerals. Licking the salt block for long stretches at a time is usually one of their favorite things to do. But if the salt block is dirty or corrupted in some way, the horse will turn his nose up at it.

As Christians, in the world, we are supposed to be salt and light. But if we lose our flavor or become corrupted with sin, we'll stop being what the world needs to function. To keep our witness and our testimony clean, we must maintain a working relationship with Christ. Prayer, Bible study, and spending time in prayer and worship will help us stay in tune with the Holy Spirit. Our focus must be on our relationship with God to keep us from becoming hypocrites and Pharisees, which are more worthless than not being a Christian in the first place. The world will turn their nose up at a false witness, so we need to stay focused.

Day 14

───

Peace I leave with you, my peace I give to you; not as the world gives do I give to you. Let not your heart be troubled, neither let it be afraid. (John 14:27)

Horses are prone to worry and anxiety. When their life is unpredictable or they are dealing with pain or stress, they can develop nervous habits like pacing and even end up with ulcers or other health related problems. It is the handler's job to notice when the horse is suffering from stress, because the horse has no voice and can't tell the handler when he is having a problem. A good handler will notice, root out the source of the problem, alleviate it, and restore peace in the horse's life. A bad handler will only treat the symptoms, such as the ulcers, and never get to the root of the problem.

The human body deals with stress in similar ways. If we allow worry and stress to overcome us, ulcers, nervous ticks, high blood pressure and other health issues are likely to occur. Often, we, like bad handlers, will treat and mask our symptoms instead of looking to the source of our lack of peace. When we focus on God, the best handler, He can provide the peace that passes all understanding. We have a voice and can tell God about our troubles and pains through prayer. He is waiting for us to bring our burdens to Him.

Day 15

The LORD himself goes before you and will be with you; he will never leave you nor forsake you. Do not be afraid; do not be discouraged. (Deuteronomy 31:8)

Horses are cautious creatures. They don't care for unpredictability, and they resist doing new things. They are afraid and readily discouraged when venturing into new territory. This is a survival instinct for them. If they aren't cautious, if they don't worry about what might be around the next corner, they might be eaten by a lion. But if they've developed a trusting relationship with their handler, then they will follow wherever the handler leads. They believe that the handler knows what she's doing, and they trust that they will be protected.

We, humans, are just as cautious when entering new territory. When we're used to things going a certain way, we balk when things suddenly change. It's hard to move on from something that may not have been the best for us to something which could be even better. If we trust in the Lord when He leads us, then we'll remember He always has our best interests at heart. He will not abandon us if a lion appears; He knows what He's doing, and we can count on His protection.

Day 16

A gentle answer turns away wrath, but a harsh word stirs up anger. (Proverbs 15:1)

Science has suggested that for each negative comment a person receives, there needs to be twenty positive comments or positive situations to overcome and repair the damage. Training a very young or feral horse is a delicate balance. The young horse needs structure, so boundaries must be set. These boundaries keep both horse and handler safe and are necessary for life lived together. At times, the horse receives punishment for bad behavior, but the punishment cannot be too harsh. The positive reinforcement should be lavished on them, or no trust can be established, and the horse will only learn fear. Remember, the horse doesn't know why the handler has set the boundaries. Nevertheless, he has to learn to respect them, even when he doesn't understand.

Likewise, God sets boundaries for us. Although His hand may feel strict at times, we have confidence in Him because He has established trust in us by showing us His love through the provision of safety. Sometimes we learn why we have certain boundaries, and sometimes we don't. We learn to respect them, even when we don't understand. We learn to trust that God has only our best in mind when we believe in His promises and understand the love He shows to us. His gentleness and kindness to us is how we develop our trust and love for Him.

Day 17

———

I, even I, am He who blots out your transgressions for My own sake; And I will not remember your sins. (Isaiah 43:25)

While establishing a rapport with a horse, the trainer must never hold a grudge. The trainer cannot get tense while going through an area where the horse spooked before. She cannot tighten her reins or choke up on the lead line. If the trainer prepares for spook or misbehavior, it has the potential to make the horse tense up and cause the very problem the trainer prepared for. And worst of all, the new horse expects the trainer to hold a grudge. He expects the trainer to punish him for behavior he hasn't even done yet, because in the horse world, horses often hold grudges against each other. A good trainer never holds grudges.

God doesn't hold a grudge against His child, either. No matter how many times we return to the same place and misbehave in the same way, He doesn't anticipate the bad behavior to happen again, with punishment at the ready. Each time we misbehave after we're forgiven, God's heart is broken like it's the first time. We may expect Him to hold grudges, because other people hold grudges against us, but God forgives us for His own sake.

Day 18

———

*B*ut the manifestation of the Spirit is given to each one for the profit of all: for to one is given the word of wisdom through the Spirit, to another the word of knowledge through the same Spirit, to another faith by the same Spirit, to another gifts of healings by the same Spirit, to another the working of miracles, to another prophecy, to another discerning of spirits, to another different kinds of tongues, to another the interpretation of tongues. But one and the same Spirit works all these things, distributing to each one individually as He wills. (I Corinthians 12:7-11)

Each horse is an individual, even within the breeds. Some Thoroughbreds are born for the track, while other Thoroughbreds are better at fox hunting, dressage, or trail riding. Not every horse will fit the mold of what a person may want to impose upon them. The gentle handler will not try to force a round peg in a square hole. The wise handler, instead, will see where the horse's potential lies and school him toward the goal where the horse has the greatest chance of success. If a horse is pressed to do a task he is not physically or mentally prepared for, frustration of both rider and trainer will prevail.

Within the church, we may see a task we wish we were better suited for. It may seem as though the teachers and preachers get all the glory while the church maintenance crew or sound assistants gets ignored. So, we may feel we'd rather take on one role more than the other. But our gifts are as they should be according to God's provision. The church needs the maintenance crew and the sound assistants just as much as any other role. Without each part of the church family, the church as a whole would not be the same. Whatever role we're called to do, we should do it with gladness, and not try to push ourselves to do something for which we aren't equipped.

Day 19

But let all those rejoice who put their trust in You; Let them ever shout for joy, because You defend them; Let those also who love Your name be joyful in You. (Psalm 5:11)

Horses in their natural state are always anxious. In the wild, their leadership can change as soon as a new horse discovers their herd. Battles between herds and leading stallions are common. Young stallions are kicked out of the herd as soon as they hit puberty and left to fend for themselves. There is no shelter from the elements. Inbreeding, famine, thirst, and predators are all commonplace. But when a horse is taken into captivity, he learns to trust his everyday handler as his leader. The handler provides food, water, safety, and constant companionship so that the horse can be set free from the anxieties of his feral life and find a happy calmness that is absent from life in the wild.

When we come to know God as our provider, we can trust that He will supply us with food, water, safety, and constant companionship, as well. If we trust that He will give us everything we need and protect us from the predators that lurk in our natural state, we'll find ourselves set free from anxiety as well. That happy calmness will come to us naturally as we learn to depend on Him with all our hearts.

Day 20

A man without self-control is like a city broken into and left without walls. (Proverbs 25:28 ESV)

Horses have very little self-control. They are ruled by their instincts for survival. Fear ignites a very strong reaction in horses, but their survival instinct also triggers a form of selfishness. They will fight each other for food and water, especially if they feel it might be scarce, or if they are the least bit hungry. Greed causes them to eat well beyond full if allowed. When in training, they learn to bypass their natural reactions. The horse can learn to hold back their fight or flight instinct, even when afraid, because they trust their trainer. Even patience at the feed trough can be learned. When the trainer stands between two horses who would normally fight over their position at the feed trough, they will respect the trainer's position and suppress the urge to bicker.

Likewise, self-control is a fruit of the Spirit. Only by leaning upon the strength of our God can we restrain what our bodies believe are natural instincts. What we *feel* like doing may not necessarily be what's best for us. God knows this, and only by trusting Him in every situation can we learn to overcome our urges. If we trust God, we can conquer our fear; we may still be afraid, but able to act in spite of it. If we remember God's position, we can withstand the need to bicker or fight with our siblings, neighbors, or co-workers. And when we believe God will provide for our every need, we can stop ourselves from over-indulging in any situation.

Day 21

Each one must give as he has decided in his heart, not reluctantly or under compulsion, for God loves a cheerful giver. (2 Corinthians 9:7 ESV)

In the English world of riding, there is hardly a more desired position for the horse to carry himself then *on-the-bit*. A horse which is on the bit is carrying himself from the hindquarters, in a round, supple shape. This horse is ready to move in any direction, to lengthen or shorten at a moment's notice, and is completely in tune with his rider. This position is best achieved through trust, time, and training. But there are many shortcuts which result in a similar, but counterfeit final product if a rider is only focused on making the horse look like he is on the bit by tucking his nose in. Typically, they all cause the horse to achieve results through coercion. The result is a nervous or unhappy horse, or one that is not truly supple and in harmony with the rider's slightest command.

God wants us to be *on-the-bit* in a similar way. The Christian should be so in-tune with God's desires, we're ready to move in any direction God wants us to at the slightest hint of his request. But if we become so focused on just being a good person, or going to church, or looking like a Christian, we'll produce only a counterfeit product, too. It's only by learning to trust the Lord, taking the time to spend with Him in prayer, and diligent study of His word, that we can truly become harmonized with our God.

Day 22

The prudent see danger and take refuge, but the simple keep going and pay the penalty. (Proverbs 22:3 NIV)

While riding a young horse, the trainer must be on the alert at all times to her surroundings. If a strange object, bicycle, person, or dog greets them on the path they take, the horse may panic when he sees the perceived danger. So, by staying alert, the trainer can be ready for the danger and avoid it as needed. But if the rider isn't alert and continues along a path which leads past a danger zone, he or she may end up on the ground when the horse shies away suddenly.

In life, we must constantly be on the alert as well. Dangers may take on different shapes and forms for us. Instead of predators, we need to avoid obvious triggers of temptation. Temptations will lead us into sin we will regret later. If the temptation can easily be avoided, then we should do what we can to escape. Being alert to what we know are problem areas for us will help us succeed in staying in communion with our Lord instead of tumbling down into a valley.

Day 23

———

When Pharaoh finally let the people go, God did not lead them along the main road that runs through Philistine territory, even though that was the shortest route to the Promised Land. God said, "If the people are faced with a battle, they might change their minds and return to Egypt." (Exodus 13:17 NLT)

When training a horse to be ridden, the trainer needs to choose her battles. Sometimes it's better to go the long way around in order to avoid a battle which will make the horse more resistant to trust the trainer. Trust must be established first. The stronger the relationship between the horse and rider, the easier these battles will be to face together. Timing is important when building a horse's trust.

God knows what battles we're ready for and which we are not. He wants to build a trusting relationship with us so that when we run into trouble, we rely upon Him instead of fighting his guiding hand. It's not that we'll never face dangers. Just as the Israelites had to face the Philistines in order to enter the promised land, we'll have great battles we need to overcome in our future as well. Even if we want to rush forward to our blessings before we're ready, God will make us wait. His timing will always coincide with our ability to trust Him.

Day 24

———

And not only that, but we also glory in tribulations, knowing that tribulation produces perseverance; and perseverance, character; and character, hope. Now hope does not disappoint, because the love of God has been poured out in our hearts by the Holy Spirit who was given to us. (Romans 5:3-5)

Different horses have different work ethics. Some are eager to please and willing to work, even looking forward to the exercise and the bonding time they have with their riders. Others are reluctant and give in only after complaining or resisting the work asked of them. Horses who do their work without begrudging it are usually quicker to move on to the next level, and thus have shorter riding sessions and are more likely to get the next day off. Horses that are resistant typically end up having to be drilled with the same task over and over before moving on. Each horse progresses at its own speed.

God is so very patient with us. There is no failure with Him. If we keep messing up the same test, He's willing to keep testing us over and over again until we pass. He expects all His children to walk, but not necessarily at the same time or at the same age. Just as each horse moves to the next level in their own time, each of God's children move up when they are ready and no sooner. He needs to spend more time with those of us who are resistant, but no matter what, He doesn't give up.

Day 25

———

A *nd let us not grow weary while doing good, for in due season* *we shall reap if we do not lose heart. (Galatians 6:9)*

In the horse show world, there is no such thing as an overnight success. Riders must be willing to take their time and teach the horse the basics without shortcuts in order to build a relationship which can withstand the pressures of competition. Trust is built little by little while doing the average, mundane tasks which come with basic flatwork and tedious repetition. But these simple exercises create a solid foundation on which a champion can be built. When a horse has obvious holes missing in its foundations, strict competition will cause the horse distress, at least, and can demolish a horse's show career at worst. The well-educated trainer will always spend as much time as is needed to build a solid foundation and rarely finds the work boring.

After his conversion on the road to Damascus, Paul spent thirteen years studying, strengthening himself in the Lord, and getting ready before making his first step in ministry. He was called to be a worker, but didn't get started until he'd done all the tedious, mundane tasks involved in building a solid foundation. If he'd taken shortcuts and left holes in his education, he would have been relying on his own strength instead of God's. Whenever a child of God tries to do this, he suffers from burn-out or even starts to question his calling because he started when he wasn't ready. But God has His own timing, and we need to work hard at trusting Him to ready us for the calling He is preparing us for.

Let us not think of the work we're doing now as boring but as necessary for our futures.

Day 26

―――――

Though he fall, he shall not be utterly cast down; For the Lord upholds him with His hand. (Psalm 37:24)

Horses can become *cast* in their stalls or pastures. A horse is said to be cast when he has lain down or rolled and managed to position himself against a wall, fence, tree, or even a hill, and he can neither get up nor reposition to roll the other way. Although normal, healthy horses lie down for several hours per day to sleep, they need to reposition themselves frequently to avoid circulation issues. In the wild, if a horse finds itself stuck in this sort of situation against a tree or hill and is unable to right himself, he could die. Under the watchful eye of the handler, the horse can be helped out of the situation before it becomes life-threatening.

What God promises us in this Psalm is that even if we fall down, we will be able to get back up again. Even if the situation is so bad that we can't get up by our own strength, He will lift us up once more. He holds our hands and keeps us from being completely cast down. We will not be stuck, and we will not die. He is ever watchful.

Day 27

---

*Y*ou provide a broad path for my feet, so that my ankles do not give way. (Psalms 18:36 NIV)

Horses have weak ankles. Actually, they don't really have ankles. Instead, n the horse has the fetlock joint. Regardless, if you look at the fact that the average horse weighs about one-thousand pounds, it's miraculous they are asked to carry this weight on ankles which are similar circumference-wise to an average human man's. This makes the horse a very delicate creature. It is easily injured, and the alert handler must be vigilant of the horse's footing. If it's too slick, the horse may slip and fall. If it's frozen, it will cause undue stress to tendons and ligaments. If it's rocky, the horse may twist a joint or get a bruise on its sole. Each change to the horse's footing should be taken into account when the horse is asked to work.

We have work to do. And God knows all our weaknesses and our faults. He also knows what kind of path lies ahead. He knows whether we can handle it or not. If we trust Him, we do not need to worry about the footing ahead because He has already made sure we will not be injured along the path He has led us upon.

Day 28

―――

*L*ove suffers long and is kind; love does not envy; love does not *parade itself, is not puffed up; does not behave rudely, does not seek its own, is not provoked, thinks no evil; does not rejoice in iniquity, but rejoices in the truth; bears all things, believes all things, hopes all things, endures all things. (1 Corinthians 13:4-7)*

The trainer must show love to the horse she is working with. She must be patient and kind and above all, understanding. While working with the horse, there is no time to show off or become too proud to put yourself in a compromising situation. The trainer should expect the best from the horse in order to show him she believes in him. When the trainer shows the horse she loves him in this way, an irrevocable trust can develop which is unlike anything the horse has ever experienced before.

God is constantly showing His love for us on a daily basis. In His word, He expresses a love we all long for, but cannot experience in this life apart from Him. Only He understands everything we're going through and has the patience to deal with our many faults and mood swings without complaint. He's never too proud to lower Himself to the deepest darkest depths of humanity in order to meet us where we are. He believes in us and knows what we're capable of, even if we don't. If we can learn to trust Him, this love is greater than the best we can imagine.

Day 29

―――

*T*hen *they said to Moses, "Because there were no graves in Egypt, have you taken us away to die in the wilderness? Why have you so dealt with us, to bring us up out of Egypt? Is this not the word that we told you in Egypt, saying, 'Let us alone that we may serve the Egyptians'? For it would have been better for us to serve the Egyptians than that we should die in the wilderness." And Moses said to the people, "Do not be afraid. Stand still, and see the salvation of the Lord, which He will accomplish for you today. For the Egyptians whom you see today, you shall see again no more forever. The Lord will fight for you, and you shall hold your peace." And the Lord said to Moses, "Why do you cry to Me? Tell the children of Israel to go forward." (Exodus 14:11-15)*

When faced with a scary object on the path, the horse's fight or flight instinct kicks in, and they want to run away as if the horse is asking, "Wouldn't it have been better if we'd never left the barn?" Many riders think this is the time to stand still, to face the fear and show the horse it's no big deal. But this is often the wrong thing to do. If a young horse is trained to stand still and face the fear, they learn to continue to make a big deal out of whatever it was they found scary. They learn it's okay to stop in the middle of work and take a look at the problem they are facing. The educated trainer does not allow the horse to stop work to look at the problem. Instead, the trainer asks the horse to continue the work, pay attention to the work, not the problem, and eventually, the horse learns to trust the trainer and loses his focus on what scared him in the first place.

When God has a task for us, but a problem arises, the first thing we often want to do is run away as well. But focusing all our energy on the problem and asking God to solve it puts too much attention on the problem. What God wants from us is to trust Him and keep working. The problem isn't as big a deal as it seems to us, and God's got it covered. As we continue forward, working on the task we've been assigned and keeping our focus on God, we'll often find out the problem isn't as big as we thought in the first place.

Day 30

Then Jesus called a little child to Him, set him in the midst of them, and said, "Assuredly, I say to you, unless you are converted and become as little children, you will by no means enter the kingdom of heaven. Therefore whoever humbles himself as this little child is the greatest in the kingdom of heaven". (Matthew 18:2-4)

"You can't teach an old dog (or horse) new tricks." The old saying is far from fact, but it does have a grain of truth in it. Older horses can be trained to do different disciplines and learn new tricks, but it may take a little longer. They may have to unlearn some automatic responses to certain aids or stimuli. With a patient trainer, the horse can regain its youthful ability to learn new things and overcome the habits which have become reflexive from its past.

When we come to the Lord, we often need to learn new tricks. It's much harder to unlearn bad habits and gain the mind of Christ if we're resistant and blaming our reflexes. If we come to God like a child, willing to learn and believing we can overcome the automatic responses we've learned, we can become His children. Only by becoming new can we learn what it means to become a child of God.

Day 31

———

*A*s God has said: *"I will dwell in them and walk among them. I will be their God, and they shall be My people." Therefore "Come out from among them and be separate," says the Lord. (2 Corinthians 6:16b-17)*

When the horse first begins work, he should be separated from the herd in order to work one on one with the trainer. Many horses suffer from severe separation anxiety during the first several training sessions. Their mind is so focused on trying to get back to the herd, they can only learn a little bit and in short spurts because they fear what will happen to them now that they are no longer hidden in the crowd. They fear predators, imaginary or not, and they fear they will no longer be able to get the sustenance they need to survive. Herd instinct is a part of their survival. But once they begin to learn to trust their trainer and accept her as their leader, they become part of a new herd made up of themselves and their trainer. Then they can concentrate fully upon their work.

New Christians sometimes have a hard time separating themselves from the crowd they once were part of. If we're focused on the world, it's almost impossible to focus on the things God has in store for us. The world hates to let us go, too. We may fear rejection; we may fear the results of separation. But once we learn more about our loving and trustworthy God, we can overcome these fears and realize there is a new relationship which is much better than any the world can provide. It's then that we're ready to work the way God wants us to.

Day 32

—————

*B*etter is a little with righteousness, than vast revenues without justice. *(Proverbs 16:8)*

The horse's stomach is relatively small for their size. It typically can hold a maximum of four gallons, but empties out once it's only 2/3 full, whether the food is fully digested or not. Because of this, it's very difficult to get horses to gain weight. The slow, methodical process of feeding the horse small amounts, several times per day is the only way to ensure the horse not only gets the most he can stomach at once, but that he's getting the proper nutrition from each meal he's fed.

Most Christians spend a quiet moment with God in the morning, but no matter how much time we spend in the morning, it won't be enough to get us through the day. Like the horse, we need little bits of God's word several times during the day in order to get the most value out of our time with God. This doesn't mean that we should give up the quality time we spend with God in the morning, but instead, consider splitting up our time a bit throughout the day to make sure we are replenishing ourselves and keeping ourselves nourished in His word and His Spirit.

Day 33

———

*N*ow, therefore, you are no longer strangers and foreigners, but fellow citizens with the saints and members of the household of God. (Ephesians 2:19)

Horses live in a herd structure. Their herd is their family. Each new horse who comes into the herd must establish their place in the structure. To become leader, the new horse would have to establish themselves as stronger and more capable than each and every member of the herd, starting at the bottom. When the capable trainer introduces herself to the herd, she must not only establish herself as the unquestionable leader, but also a part of the family structure. If the trainer is not considered part of the family, it is much more difficult to develop the bonds of trust needed to give each horse the training and care they require.

When we become members of the household of God, He becomes a part of our family—not just a member of our family, but the undisputed head of the household. But as family, we must learn to trust Him as more capable and stronger than anyone who has lead us before and even more capable than we are of taking care of us, ourselves. Much of what we thought was necessary in caring for ourselves we'll learn is less effective than God's methods of doing things. It's only by accepting His leadership and trusting Him as family that we can learn to become true children of God.

Day 34

---

*L*ord, you alone are my portion and my cup; you make my lot se-cure. The boundary lines have fallen for me in pleasant places; surely I have a delightful inheritance. (Psalm 16:5-6)

Even if a well-handled horse has been trained to jump obstacles higher than the fence which contains their pasture, he will rarely jump out. Wild horses see fencing as obstacles. Fences are in the way of their freedom. They will either fear the fence and panic, because they can no longer go in their desired direction, or they will jump it. Once a wild horse is trained, it learns that fencing is not only there to keep them contained, but also for their safe-ty. The world outside the fence is much more dangerous than the world within it. Many dangers are kept out because of the fenc-ing as well. The horses learn their boundaries contain a pleasant place.

God places boundaries upon us as well. Do we see them as ob-stacles which keep us from having the same fun the world is hav-ing? Or do we see them as guardrails which keep us safe from the harm which could befall us from jumping over them? He gives us rules and sets up borders because He knows the dangers wrong choices contain. When we're young and wild, we often get an immortality complex. People warn us about the dangers of the things we want to do, but we've seen others who didn't become addicted to those drugs or didn't lose all their money through gambling. So many young people rush headlong into those dan-gers because they think the side-effects won't happen to them.

But there are always prices to pay for crossing boundaries. If we stay within the confines God has created to keep us safe, we soon learn they contain the most pleasant of places.

Day 35

In peace I will both lie down and sleep; for you alone, O Lord, make me dwell in safety. (Psalm 4:8)

For several hours per day, horses lie flat out in order to get deep sleep. But if they live alone and have no other horses to watch over them, they often don't feel safe enough to lie down and get the sleep they need. One exception to this is when a horse is kept in their stall for part of the day; they feel safety in the borders provided by the walls. Because their daily handler has been established as the head of their herd, they feel safe because they know the handler is close by.

God provides a safe place for us to rest. We can rest knowing He is close by. If we let the cares of this world overwhelm us, or we know we have broken the boundaries of life God has placed upon us, we may lose the ability to rest in safety. By doing this, we reject Him for the sake of something we think we want more. When we embrace the life God has given us and live in close communion with Him, then we can trust His presence as a loving father. This is the only way to be at peace.

Day 36

———

Likewise you younger people, submit yourselves to your elders. Yes, all of you be submissive to one another, and be clothed with humility, for "God resists the proud, but gives grace to the humble." (1 Peter 5:5)

Horses at the uppermost level of competition are completely yielded to their riders. They do not argue with the rider's guiding hand. Because of the relationship of trust built between the two, the horse understands that the rider will not ask for something beyond his capabilities. He trusts the rider will not push him to heights he cannot conquer. The horse believes his rider has his best interests at heart, and that submission is the best and easiest way for happiness in their relationship.

Proud people believe their own way is best. Their feelings and rationality are the most important, and they know better than anyone else what is right for themselves. They wrestle with God just like Jacob did in chapter thirty-two of Genesis. But when we are humble, we receive God's grace in a new way. When we yield to Him as freely and easily as leaves on the wind, we can conquer new heights and develop a happier, more trusting relationship with our Master.

Day 37

The Lord of hosts has sworn, saying, "Surely, as I have thought, so it shall come to pass, and as I have purposed, so it shall stand" (Isaiah 14:24)

Before going into each riding session, the rider must determine both short-term goals (what needs to be accomplished today) as well as long-term goals. Visualizing those goals make them easier to reach. When working with the horse, the time limits for these goals may have to change based on how fast the horse learns, weather conditions, and other obstacles. But provided the rider is determined, takes things as slowly as the horse needs her to, and keeps the goals realistic, they will come to pass.

God knows us better than we even know ourselves. He has both short-term goals and long-term goals for us. He shows us visions of what we are to become so we have some idea as to where we're heading. He's patient and knows how long it's going to take us to learn the things we need to know before accomplishing our vision. God is more determined and patient than we could ever imagine, and when He has a goal for us to meet, it will come to pass, even if it's not on our time schedule.

Day 38

———

But let your 'Yes' be 'Yes,' and your 'No,' 'No.' For whatever is more than these is from the evil one. (Matthew 5:37)

A horse must have consistency in its training. What the handler says "no" to a behavior today, it must still be "no" tomorrow. If the owner is lax in the horse's training, and punishes behavior one day, but fails to punish it the next, the horse will get confused and find the times when it's punished are unfair. If it's okay to do something once, it should always be okay. Each time the horse is handled, it is learning something new. If the handler sets specific boundaries of right behavior and wrong behavior, or good reactions to cues and bad reactions to stubbornness, the horse will learn faster and without frustration.

As we've grown up as children of God, we feel the same way. A parent that says it's okay to do something before, but then punishes later for the same action is immediately viewed as unfair and unjust. This is why God is said to be the same yesterday, today, and forever (Hebrews 13:8). If He changed His mind based on popular opinion or what is politically correct, then He would be an unjust God. If we learn God's boundaries for our lives, we can rest assured they will not change. This helps us to learn without frustration as well.

Day 39

───

She equips herself with strength [spiritual, mental, and physical fitness for her God-given task] And makes her arms strong. (Proverbs 31:17 AMP)

Competition horses must be fit for the task they are asked to perform. The educated trainer will make certain the horse is ready, both physically and mentally, for the tasks she asks. If the horse is not prepared, it can be injured. Physical injury such as ligament tears and pulled tendons are common when the horse has not been strengthened for competition. Mental injuries are even more difficult for the horse to overcome. Some horses pushed to jump bigger and bigger before they are mentally ready will have one crash and then refuse to ever jump again. Horses each grow stronger at different paces. It's the trainer's job to move forward at the pace which allows the horse to recover from small failures.

God's patience is longsuffering. He is in no hurry to make us do more than we're ready for. Although He may give us a vision of doing great and glorious things, He doesn't expect us to do them without being ready for them. Each time we go through a small test and pass it, we're gaining the strength we need to get ready for the big test. If we fail a small test, God doesn't give up on us, and we must learn how to bounce back from small failures so we don't give up and refuse to move forward again. God has great plans for us if we prepare ourselves at His pace.

Day 40

Your word is a lamp to my feet and a light to my path. (Psalm 119:105)

Horses have superior night vision to humans. In the wild, most predators are active primarily at night. This means the horse must be vigilant, able to see predators as they approach, and ready to run at full speed over uneven terrain, using only the stars and moonlight for help to see the path in front of them. Their eyes are designed with greater numbers of rods than cones, and their retinas have a reflective structure around them allowing them to use the miniscule amount of light to their best advantage. Studies have shown horses can determine shapes and see obstacles even in the most dimly lit situations.

God's word is the source of our light. The reason we're able to walk through the valley of the shadow of death is because no matter how dark things are, God's word is there to help us and be a light to show us the way out of those situations. Even if our Bible is not with us at the time, God has provided us with recall through His Spirit in times of need. Sometimes just one verse remembered at the most opportune time can give us all of the comfort and light we need to cling to in a dim situation.

Conclusion

———

I've been working with horses for almost thirty years. During my time with them, I've learned so much about myself as well as how to work with these majestic animals and the people in my lives. When I'm communing with God while I work, I learned short little anecdotes and wrote them down over the years. That's how this short devotional came to be.

Thank you for taking this journey with me. If you'd like to continue the journey to having a closer walk with our Trainer, God, please continue reading for a prayer and study guide.

~Pauline

———

THE CHRISTIAN'S PERSONAL TRINITY

I submit that your personal trinity is: Prayer, Bible Reading, Praise.

SO NOW ARRIVES THE question that will help us choose whether to continue reading this book or not. Do you want change? Do you want it enough in your life to change your habits and spend more time with the One who can make your life one worth loving?

PRAY THROUGH YOUR EMOTIONS

Let's remember first, we don't need to put on a front with God. We don't need to hide our feelings from Him – He already knows how we feel. We don't need to pretend to be something we are not —He already knows who we are.

I hope that you just took a sigh of relief when you realized God doesn't want us to pretend with Him – He wants our honesty. Look at the prayers peppered throughout the Old Testament, and you'll see a common thread – "Why?"

Why do You stand afar off, O Lord? Why do You hide in times of trouble? (Psalm 10:1)

I will say to God, my Rock, "Why have you forgotten me? Why do I go mourning because of the oppression of the enemy?" (Psalm 42:9)

Why do You hide Your face, and forget our affliction and our oppression? (Psalm 44:24)

Have you ever felt like that? Why aren't you here God? Why don't you care that I'm having trouble in my life? Why don't you see what I'm going through?

Realize this – our anger with God does not drive a wedge between us and Him. It is our silence that drives the wedge. Your relationship with God is the same as your relationship with your spouse in this way. If you don't talk to each other and voice your problems, allowing the other to comfort you or tell you why, then you will be driven apart rather than together.

When you are angry or confused in your life and wonder where God is, ask Him. Don't ask someone else, ask HIM. And don't take silence as a response. Pour it all out to Him, over and over again if necessary.

> *In those days, I, Daniel, was mourning three full weeks. I ate no pleasant food, no meat or wine came into my mouth, nor did I anoint myself at all, till three whole weeks were fulfilled. Now on the twenty-fourth day of the first month, as I was by the side of the great river, that is, the Tigris, I lifted my eyes and looked, and behold, a certain man clothed in linen, whose waist was girded with gold of Uphaz! (Daniel 10:2-5)*

> *Then he said to me, "Do not fear, Daniel, for from the first day that you set your heart to understand, and to humble yourself before your God, your words were*

heard; and I have come because of your words. But the prince of the kingdom of Persia withstood me twenty-one days; and behold, Michael, one of the chief princes came to help me." (Daniel 10:12-13)

Daniel prayed and fasted for three weeks before getting an answer. But he persisted, and he had faith God would answer. Please note the fact that God sent the answer right away, but the messenger was delayed by Satan and his wiles.

If Satan can get us to give up by delaying the message—rest assured that he will do it. His entire goal in keeping us from the change we need is to get us to doubt that God can do it, that He wants to do it, or that He loves us enough to do it. If we quit, Satan wins.

Falling is not failure. It's part of the process. If you mess up or fall down, trust God and get back up. It's when you stay down and quit that you lose.

That's what the "silent treatment" does in your relationship with God. It's when we give up and stop talking to Him because we just don't see the *use*. As long as we keep yelling and railing at God, asking Him why, and being open and honest with Him—we will strengthen that relationship.

PRAY THROUGH YOUR DOUBT

Then Moses answered and said, "But suppose they will not believe me or listen to my voice; suppose they say, 'The Lord has not appeared to you.'"

So the Lord said to him, "What is that in your hand?

He said "A Rod."

And He said, "Cast it on the ground." So he cast it on the ground and it became a serpent; and Moses fled from it.

Then the Lord said to Moses, "Reach out your hand and take it by the tail" (and he reached out his hand and caught it, and it became a rod in his hand), "that they may believe that the Lord God of their fathers, the God of Abraham, the God of Isaac, and the God of Jacob, has appeared to you."

Furthermore, the Lord said to him, "Now put your hand in your bosom." And he put his hand in his bosom, and when he took it out, behold, his hand was leprous, like snow.

And He said, "Put your hand in your bosom again." So he put his hand in his bosom again, and drew it out of his bosom, and behold, it was restored like his other flesh. "Then it will be if they do not believe you, nor heed the message of the first sign, that they may believe the latter sign. And it shall be that if they do not believe even these two signs or listen to your voice, that you shall take water from the river and pour it on the dry land. The water which you take from the river will become blood on dry land."

Then Moses said to the Lord, "O my Lord, I am not eloquent, neither before nor since You have spoken to Your servant; but I am slow of speech and slow of tongue."

So the Lord said to him, "Who has made man's mouth? Or who makes the mute, the deaf, the seeing or the blind? Have not I, the Lord? Now therefore, go and I will be your mouth and teach you what you shall say."

But he said, "O my Lord, please send by the hand of whomever else You may send."

So the anger of the Lord was kindled against Moses, and He said: "Is not Aaron the Levite your brother? I know that he can speak well. And look, he is coming out to meet you. When he sees you, he will be glad in his heart. Now you shall speak to him and put the words in his mouth. And I will be with your mouth and with his mouth, and I will teach you what you shall do." (Exodus 4:1-15)

This was Moses praying through his doubt. God spoke to Moses and told him what He wanted Moses to do. But Moses was too scared to move, too unsure of himself to go where God told him to go and change what God told him to change. So he faced every doubt in prayer (talking to God) and God brought him through to trusting Him in every instance.

Moses was afraid people wouldn't believe him, so God gave him miraculous signs for proof. Moses had a stutter and was afraid of speaking publicly, soGod assured him that he could be healed.

Moses didn't want to do the job alone, so God let his brother go with him.

We don't have to face our fears alone. We don't have to hide our doubts. God wants us to expose our doubts and fears to the light of His mercy and grace. It is in that light that He can show we have no reason to fear or doubt.

But do you still doubt?

Remember the story about the man whose son was demon possessed, and the disciples couldn't cast it out? The father doubted Jesus could do anything, either. And yet, even though he was full of doubt, he had hope that Jesus could do it.

The Father said: "But if You can do anything, have compassion on us and help us."

Jesus said to him, "If you can believe, all things are possible to him who believes." Immediately the father of the child cried out and said with tears, "Lord, I believe; help my unbelief!" (Mark 9:22-24)

That was a prayer that Jesus gladly answered. Again, silence would not help this man, only prayer. When we doubt that God can do what we need, just pray this simple prayer. Tell God what you believe. Tell Him that you want to believe more. Then be faithful in what you know you can do.

Sometimes we will be required to take a leap of faith. Have you seen *Indiana Jones and the Last Crusade*? Toward the end of the movie, Indy has to pass three tests in order to gain the Holy Grail and save his father's life. The final test in this series is the "Leap of Faith." Indy has to walk in faith across a canyon to the other side.

He doesn't want to do it. He can see that if he steps off the ledge that he will fall to his death. The canyon seems bottomless. But Indy also knows what his book says, and it says that if he has faith and steps off the lion's head, he will make it to the other side.

So this is where we might find ourselves. Our book says that if we have faith we'll make it to the other side, but we can see that the cavern is deep and that the fall will kill us. It's time to pray that prayer of help for our unbelief – and then have the faith to take that first step.

That is the moment of truth. The father in the previous story took that first step and then found himself across the canyon of belief to a healed son without effort beyond that initial tread. Jesus did the remainder. But what if he didn't pray that prayer or trust that Jesus could even help his unbelief? He would never have made it across that canyon or found his son's healing.

Indy also found that the first step took faith, but every other step afterward was a breeze. Under his feet he found a hidden walkway that couldn't be seen from the edge of the cliff. If you only believe in what you see, that's not faith. God wants us to take the first step for our freedom in faith, praying through our doubt. Then we will find that our doubt was unfounded and our faith grounded.

PRAYING THROUGH TO CHANGE

God moves through people. Good luck is when God chooses to move anonymously. Sometimes we seem to luck into what we desire, but most of the time God works through people. God assures us that even people like these pillars of faith, trees of belief, and towers of holiness, are *people* just like us.

> *The earnest (heartfelt, continued) prayer of a righteous man makes tremendous power available (dynamic in its working). Elijah was a human being with a nature such as we have (with feelings, affections, and a constitution like ours): and he prayed earnestly for it not to rain and no rain fell on the earth for three years and six months. (James 5:17-18 AMP)*

Elijah had emotions he had to pray through. He had doubts and needed to take leaps of faith. But God was with him and when he prayed for change, whether it was rain or no rain, change happened.

When we bring all our doubts and fears to God, we'll find the reason to trust Him. And as we trust Him, we will draw closer to Him. Best of all, no one who draws closer to God can possibly remain unchanged.

Take a look at the "heroes" of the Bible. God specializes in making people into the opposite of what they once were. Abraham had no children, but God made him the "Father of Many Nations." Gideon was a coward, but God made him one of the mightiest generals of all time. David was the smallest, most insignificant boy in all of Bethlehem, but God made him king. Peter was an uneducated fisherman, but God made him into the "foundation" of the church. Saul persecuted Christians, but God made him into the encourager of the brethren. And there's more than just these few!

The world loves to label people. This one's ADHD; that one has OCD; he's a control freak; she's hereditarily obese. But none of these labels matter to God. He's interested in making a change in us that makes those labels obsolete. God loves to do this because when He makes you into the opposite of what the world says you are, it proves that only He could do it!

So what change do you need to make? What doubts and fears do you have? Bring it all to God, and let Him prove to you the power of prayer to make change and set free.

POSITION YOURSELF IN THE WORD

In order to set us free, God needs us ready for battle. The sword of truth is the only offensive weapon that we have in our arsenal. This is why it's so important to have a daily Bible reading time.

Positioning ourselves for battle is a decision that we must make; it will not happen as a result of our inactivity. We cannot get the Bible through osmosis. We have to pick it up and read it. Even reading it is not enough. It's studying it and applying it to our lives that changes us from captive to free person.

THE IMPORTANCE OF BIBLE LITERACY

There are so many ways to avoid reading the Bible today, and many of them have the appearance of good. We can listen to praise music, or Bible teaching tapes, we can read good "Christian Living Guides" or "Daily Devotionals." But none of these are quite the same as just picking up your Bible and reading.

Why is that? When we are listening to praise music, teaching tapes, devotionals, and Christian books, we are seeing the Word from the point of view of the person who is speaking or writing. Although God can and will use these things for His purposes, we are still using an interpreter that is not the Holy Spirit.

God wants to speak to you without an interpreter.

For this commandment which I command you today is not too mysterious for you, nor is it far off. It is not in heaven, that you should say, "Who will ascend into heaven for us and bring it to us that we may hear and do it?"

Nor is it beyond the sea that you should say, "Who will go over the sea for us and bring it to us, that we may hear it and do it? But the word is very near you, in your mouth and in your heart, that you may do it. (Deuteronomy 30:11-14 NKJV)

Notice God said in the first sentence that the Bible is NOT too mysterious for you. D. L. Moody said: "The devil wants us to believe we will never understand religion or God, or the Bible or Jesus. Would Christ have made a child the standard of faith if He had known it was not capable of understanding His words?"

If you are having trouble reading God's word, then find a different version! I was raised in a Southern Baptist church – one that only advocated use of the King James 1611 Version of the Bible. For the next twelve years, after being saved and baptized, I continuously tried to read the Bible, and failed miserably each time. The words seemed old, archaic, and useless for me today.

Then when I was about twenty-five years old, I found *The Message* version by Eugene Peterson. My eyes were opened! I have now read the Bible from cover to cover at least five times. And I have read it in four different versions (The Message, NIV, NKJV, The Living Bible, and currently AMP). When judged by a single-version-only person for my freedom, I remember what Paul said:

For why is my liberty judged by another man's conscience? But if I partake with thanks, why am I evil spoken of for the food over which I give thanks? (1 Corinthians 10:29-30 NKJV)

God's word is food. It is described in the Bible as bread and meat. When we read the Bible, our soul is being fed with the nutrition and vitamins we need to grow spiritually. When we are trying to get our nutrients through only praise, books, teaching, and devotionals, it's like trying to live on fast food. It keeps you from starving but might stunt your growth!

If I didn't read the word of God regularly, I wouldn't hear Him speak to me so clearly. His word truly makes me grow in faith and have the encouragement that I need to change and be free.

There are so many times when I open my Bible and Satan whispers to me, "How are you going to get anything out of Jeremiah? He's so depressing." Or "Luke sure is long-winded and you've read this chapter fifty times—you're wasting your time."

He is a liar, and God proves it every time. I pray on each occasion that God will face up to those lies and prove Satan wrong by giving me a special word in my reading that I can use *today*! God always comes through.

Isn't it time to let God come through for you? Pray before you read the Bible, and if you're having a hard time understanding the version you are using, find one that speaks to your heart.

HOW IS THE BIBLE RELEVANT TODAY?

Once we've gotten a Bible that we genuinely understand when we read it—and have said a prayer before starting—what is the plan? Do you start at Genesis 1:1 and read a chapter or two each day until you reach Revelations 23:21? For me, this idea is boring, and I can't abide it. I can't stay tuned in to the word everyday if I do things this way. For you it might work, but it doesn't for me.

Granted, I'm also the kind of person who reads more than one book at a time. If one has a boring section, then I only read a chapter or so at a time until the pace picks up. So that's what I do with my Bible. I have five bookmarks in my Bible, because I have split it up into five sections. I read a chapter from each section per day until that section is done, and then start all over again.

Section 1: Genesis – Esther

Section 2: Job – Song of Solomon

Section 3: Isaiah – Malachi

Section 4: Matthew – Acts

Section 5: Romans – Revelation

Job through Song of Solomon in the Old Testament is considered the "poetry and allegory" section. It is book-ended by books of history. So that is why the Old Testament is split up into three parts the way that I have it. The New Testament is split up so that I have separated the Gospels and Acts from the Letters of the Apostles.

If you follow my reading plan, you'll finish the entire Bible within one year even if you miss a day or two now and then. More importantly, you won't be bored by Deuteronomy or Leviticus and quit. You'll discover which book is your favorite, (Isaiah is mine) and you'll find that there are passages every day that interact with each other in the Old and New Testaments in fresh and interesting ways.

Another method is to read a chapter or two of the Old Testament and a chapter or two of the New. This is a perfectly acceptable method also.

Regardless of how you decide to delve into the word of God, what is most important is how you read it. First, you must understand that almost every promise in the Bible can apply to your life in some way. When God says in *Isaiah 54:1 – For more are the children of the desolate than the children of the married woman, Says the Lord,* He's not just talking about Sarah here. He may be talking to you.

Now the reason I said "may be talking to you" is simple. As you pray and read through God's word, the Holy Spirit will speak to your heart. He will tell you which promises are yours and which are not. You cannot claim the promises that are not meant for you. When God tells Abraham that He *"will make him the father of many nations," (Genesis 17:4),* you cannot decide that this promise is for you by naming it and claiming it.

Several of the promises are yours, as they are for EVERY believer: *"Believe on the Lord Jesus Christ, and you will be saved, you and your household." (Acts 16:31)* This verse is a personal favorite of mine, because if you have an unsaved father, husband, daughter, son – God promises that your whole household will be saved, because you will pray them into salvation through your obedience to the Holy Spirit. Isn't that awesome?

Then some of the promises of God are personally yours to claim. But no matter what, you have to read the Bible taking into account that it is not LITERAL all the time. Sometimes it can be applied to your situation without being taken out of context.

For example, take a look at 1 Corinthians 10:23: *All things are lawful for me, but not all things are helpful; all things are lawful for me, but not all things edify. Let no one seek his own, but each one the other's well-being.*

This passage does not refer only to food and idols, but also to any other "sin" that a person makes up for themselves that does not necessarily apply to everyone. For example, if I find that playing video games distracts me from my life with Jesus, then I can discover playing video games is a "sin" for me. But if I then say that playing video games is a sin for everyone, I am wrong.

Yes, Paul declared all things lawful for me. But this does not mean that I should continue in sin so that grace can abound (see Romans 8). If we want to be happy in Jesus, we need to be tuned into the Holy Spirit and God's word constantly through prayer and diligent study. It is only by following where the Holy Spirit guides us that we will see freedom in our lives.

This also means that when God talked to Sarah, Jacob, Joshua, Gideon, Peter, or Paul, God might also be talking to you. It is equally true at times when He is talking to the WHOLE nation of Israel that He's talking to you:

> *But now, thus says the Lord, who created you, O Jacob, and He who formed you, O Israel: "Fear not, for I have*

redeemed you; I have called you by your name; You are Mine.

When you pass through the waters, I will be with you and through the rivers, they shall not overflow you. When you walk through the fire, you shall not be burned, Nor shall the flame scorch you. (Isaiah 43:1-2)

"You are My witnesses," says the Lord, "And my servant whom I have chosen, that you may know and believe Me, and understand that I am He. Before Me there was no God formed, Nor shall there be after Me. I even I, am the Lord, and besides Me there is no savior. (Isaiah 43:10-11)

If you understand that God isn't just talking to Israel when He said this, but He's talking to you and to me, then you will understand why my favorite book of the Bible is Isaiah. I honestly hope that you are seeing the word of God in the light which it was intended. God is the Great Physician, and His word is the balm of healing. There is nothing that is happening to you now that is not mentioned in His word. He is waiting for you to listen and be healed. He must heal you to set you free.

BECOMING BATTLE READY

"There is no neutral ground in the universe; every square inch, every split second, is claimed by God and counter claimed by Satan." – C. S. Lewis

Satan knows the word of God better than almost anyone.

Ninety-nine times out of one hundred, the Holy Spirit talks to my heart with a direct quote of scripture. But Satan knows scripture, too. Remember when Jesus fasted for 40 days in the wilderness, and Satan came to tempt Him? Satan quoted scripture during the second temptation:

(Satan) said to Him, "If you are the Son of God, throw Yourself down. For it is written: 'He shall give His angels charge over you,' and 'In their hands they shall bear you up, Lest you dash your foot against a stone.'"

Jesus said to (Satan), "It is written also, 'You shall not tempt the Lord your God.'" (Matthew 4:6-7)

So how did Jesus know that the word that Satan was naming wasn't for Him to claim at this time? Fasting brings the believer closer to God and increases faith. To abstain from food for this length of time would require His intervention. His intervention comes through prayer. Jesus already knew His mission and knew that the scripture Satan tempted Him with was against His prior calling.

If we are constantly in touch with God through prayer and study, we will know God's will for our lives and will not be confused by the wiles of the devil. This is why we pray, study, and meditate on the Word. If you don't know God's word, you won't know what to do when Satan comes. In fact, you may not even recognize him as Satan.

For the word of God is living and powerful, and sharper than any two-edged sword, piercing even to the division of the soul and spirit, and of the joints and marrow, and is a discerner of the thoughts and intents of the heart. (Hebrews 4:12)

Whose heart does it discern? It discerns your heart as you read, through conviction, understanding, and encouragement. But it also discerns between the heart of God and the heart of Satan. Satan cannot successfully lie to you when you are deep in the scriptures.

The more we study, the longer our sword. Satan loves when we only have a cursory knowledge of the word of God. Because when our sword is short, we can be reached easier. He loves when you know enough to recognize the word, but not enough to discern it utterly. When he "kind of" quotes scripture, but twists it for his purposes, we need to know enough of the word to counter it the way Jesus did, or we may fall for his plot of temptation.

Now the serpent was more cunning than any beast of the field which the Lord God had made. And he said to the woman, "Has God indeed said, 'you shall not eat of every tree of the garden'?"

And the woman said to the serpent, "We may eat of the fruit of the trees of the garden; but of the fruit of the tree which is in the midst of the garden, God has said, 'you shall not eat it, nor shall you touch it, lest you die.'"

Then the serpent said to the woman, "You will not surely die. For God knows that in the day you eat of it your eyes will be opened, and you will be like God, knowing good and evil." (Genesis 3:1-4)

But here's what God actually said:

"Of every tree of the garden you may freely eat; but of the tree of the knowledge of good and evil you shall not eat, for in the day that you eat of it you shall surely die." (Genesis 2:16-17)

Eve changed God's word. She added: "nor shall you touch it." So many people of God who have a cursory knowledge of His word will add commandments to the word of God that God did not place upon them. They think that they will be better and holier by obeying what they have decided God said.

This is called living under the law. It places a burden upon us that is greater than the "easy" burden that Jesus promised. When we add more to the load that we carry, it becomes harder to carry the load that Jesus placed on us. This makes it easier to shirk off and give up.

It saddens me greatly when people tell me they "tried" Christianity but found it too cumbersome. They couldn't follow all of the rules, so they quit. They tell me they see God as a rule-monger who sends people to Hell for not worshipping Him. And they do not understand when I say that God helps me to overcome my self-condemnation and gives me a greater self-worth. They can't comprehend that He is the God of encouragement who changes me.

What if they haven't read the whole Bible for themselves? Because the language is "archaic," they may have believed that they could not understand the Bible for themselves. God did not mean for us to hear His words through the thoughts of others. When we do that, it's as if we are playing the elementary school "telephone" game.

I'm sure you've played it, but just in case: it's where there is a long line of kids. The first kid whispers in the ear of the second. The second kid whispers into the third. And so it goes until you reach the other end. Then the last kid says whatever he/she was told out loud. Usually it's nothing like what the first kid said. That's what makes the game both fun and funny.

We don't want to play the "telephone" game with God's word. Doing that causes it to lose its power and makes it easier for Satan to distort. We need to go directly to the source in study and prayer so that we will have our full armor and become battle ready.

This treatise is a response to people who neglect any portion of our personal trinity because they think they get enough from one of the others. I do not mean to say that you should stop listening to Bible teaching, but I do say that you will not grow the way that you could unless you ALSO read God's word for yourself.

So are you battle ready? Can you discern the difference between God's command and Satan's temptation? Every day we need to remember that there is no neutral ground in this war, and it's on our doorstep – not on foreign soil. Let us sharpen our minds, hearts, and our Sword so we will be ready for battle.

Do you need P.O.W.E.R .?

Praise may seem useless to some, but could it be the source of power we seek?

We need the power of God in our lives if He is to free us from our fears. If we want the power of God, there is one part of our personal trinity that cannot be neglected, and that's praise. Here's an acronym to remember:

For P.O.W.E.R. you need:

Praise

Oriented

Worship

Experienced

Regularly

The Psalms are full of praise – why do you think David was a man after God's own heart? There was hardly another man with more of the power of God in his life than David. Let's look at something, and this one really gets to me:

Then David danced before the Lord with all his might, clad in a linen ephad. So David and all the house of Israel brought up the ark of the Lord with shouting and with the sound of the trumpet. (2 Samuel 6:14-15)

And though so many of God's people joined in the celebration and blessing, one person disapproved— his wife Michal.

Then David returned to bless his household. And Michal, the daughter of Saul came out to meet David, and said, "How glorious was the king of Israel today, uncovering himself today in the eyes of the maids of his servants, as one of the base fellows shamelessly uncovers himself!"

So David said to Michal, "It was before the Lord, who chose me instead of your father and all his house, to appoint me ruler over the people of the Lord, over Israel. Therefore I will play music before the Lord. And I will be even more undignified than this, and will be humble in my own sight. But as for the maidservants of whom you have spoken, by them I will be held in honor." (2 Samuel 6:21-22)

A praise song, "Undignified, shows David's response. David's praise is the kind God is looking for. He wants us to be so free in our love for Him that we would be willing to look undignified. And although all of Israel was blessed by David's praising and shouting, Michal died barren. Whether that's because David refused to touch her or if God closed her womb, who knows?

Here's another big revelation of praise's power:

So the people shouted when the priests blew the trumpets. And it happened when the people heard the sound of the trumpet, and the people shouted with a great shout, that the wall fell down flat. Then the people went up into the city, every man straight before him, and they took the city. (Joshua 6:20)

Trumpets blowing, God's people shouting = praising! And what kind of power was held in that praise? The power to tear down walls! Aren't there walls in your life that need tearing down? The walls of depression, fear, or addiction can overwhelm us. All of them can be torn down when God's people give every portion of our personal trinity the attention it deserves.

When we trust God, listen to Him, and praise Him, change occurs within us naturally. He promised that He came so that we could live in abundance. He does not want us to lead a life of self-condemnation. Have you ever listened to worship music and wished you could have that kind of relationship with God? Well I am telling you that you can! Let Him defeat the condemnation in your life, too.

Praise is a faith catalyst. It activates our faith and tunes us into God through our mind and emotions, reaching down to our very soul. There's a Bible story illustrating the great connection of prayer, praise, and power. When King Jehoshaphat was surrounded by an army that greatly outnumbered him, he tapped into God's awesome power with prayer and praise. He prayed to God, and this is what God answered:

You will not need to fight in this battle. Position yourselves, stand still and see the salvation of the Lord, who is with you, O Judah and Jerusalem! Do not fear or be dismayed: tomorrow go out against them for the Lord is with you. And Jehoshaphat bowed his head with his face to the ground, and all Judah and the inhabitants of Jerusalem bowed before the Lord, worshipping the Lord. (2 Chronicles 20:17-18)

So what is *our* battle plan? The enemy is before us and he's tempting us with fear. Do we fight him first and then turn to the Lord? King Jehoshaphat didn't fight without turning toward the Lord. In verse 20:3, He proclaimed a fast throughout all Judea, and sought the Lord, *first*.

First Step: Pray. Take it to God in prayer. Declare to Him that you see and understand your weakness, and that if He doesn't fight the battle for you, then you will fail. Give it up to Him, every part, and don't try to do what you can't do. Give all of it up to His strength.

Second Step: Position yourself and Stand Still. Do not try to do anything. Do not fight what you can't. Do not try this or that to remedy the situation. And do not distract yourself with something else – or the "something else" might become a golden calf. Stand still, pray, and wait.

Third Step: Do Not Fear! Trust God. The enemy may seem strong, but the Lord is there with you, and He is stronger. All you have to do is trust and lean upon Him.

Last Step: Worship Him.

Worship and trust—we can hardly have one without the other. True worship can only come when we believe and trust God. And when we do that, worship will naturally flow from our hearts. When the battle is too much for you, do not surrender to the enemy— surrender to God. He will give you the strength you need to withstand the forces against you. Trust and He will give you reason to praise Him. For contained within that praise is the power to make a change in your life toward freedom.

FINAL NOTE

Prayer, positioning yourself in the word, and worshiping in praise is God's battle plan for us. The sooner we realize that life is not meant to be perfect and easy all the time, but instead it's a battle, the more enjoyable life will become. Seems ironic? It's all about mindset. If we think life should be easy, we become unhappy when it's not. But if we realize it's a battle, we can find joy in small victories.

Keep fighting the battles, and God will make you victorious.

I hope that reading this book has helped you to see some facet of our life in Jesus in a new way.

If you have been moved by this work, please leave a review or connect with me on Facebook: http://facebook.com/PaulineCreeden

———————————

Please continue for a sneak peek of

FREEDOM FROM FEAR

INTRODUCTION

FEAR IS A CAGE. IT closes us in and keeps us from living in freedom. Some people get so overcome by fear that they cannot even leave their house. Phobias have become almost fashionable. We label our fears and hug them tight to us as if they are things we need to keep. We coddle them and keep them happy so that they don't destroy us. The last thing we want to do is provoke them.

That powerlessness keeps us from accomplishing great things in our lives, whether personally or for God's kingdom. In this Bible study, we're going to work through the ways to increase our faith and walk in obedience – the keys to our freedom from fear.

We must believe that Jesus can and will help us to overcome. Too often we have faith, but not enough. We are like the father from Mark 9 who brought his demon possessed son to Jesus, saying "If you can do anything, won't you please take pity on us and help us?"

If He can. Our faith tends to stop there because we've lost our ability to trust. *If* He can, *if* He will, *if* He'll care enough to take a look. But Jesus said in answer, "*If* you can believe, all things are possible to those who believe." So the question is, do we believe, and if we believe, how do we act upon that belief?

Each believer develops their own personal faith in Jesus – their *own* relationship with Him. He's not the friend of a friend, your father's friend, or your mother's, but yours. And as your friend,

He has given you several promises. To overcome fear, we have to take Him at his word: believe and then act in obedience to what we believe.

FAITH THAT OVERCOMES FEAR

We have to learn to trust Jesus in the midst of life's circumstances.

FAITH OVERCOMES THE three main causes of fear. We fear because we don't like when things are out of our control. We feel afraid when we feel alone. In the face of our trials, we fear because we feel helpless to change our circumstances.

- Circumstances beyond our control
  - Being completely alone
  - Helpless in the face of trials

On the same day, when evening had come, He said to them, "Let us cross over to the other side." Now when they had left the multitude, they took Him along in the boat as He was. And other little boats were also with Him. And a great windstorm arose, and the waves beat into the boat, so that it was already filling. But He was in the stern, asleep on a pillow. And they awoke Him and said to Him, "Teacher, do You not care that we are perishing?"

Then He arose and rebuked the wind, and said to the sea, "Peace, be still!" And the wind ceased and there was a great calm. But He said to them, "Why are you so fearful? How is it that you have no faith?" And they feared exceedingly, and said to one another, "Who can this be, that even the wind and the sea obey Him!" (Mark 4:32-41)

DO YOU FEAR BEING OUT OF CONTROL?

The disciples had Jesus in their boat. But when the storms came up and threatened their lives, they were filled with fear. They ran to Jesus, and woke Him, wondering if Jesus even cared that they were dying. Their faith in Jesus did not measure up to their fear of the storm.

They momentarily forgot that Jesus was in control.

Everyone faces trials. It's the result of the fallen world we live in. Even if it's smooth sailing right now, it's only a matter of time before a storm comes up and rocks the boat. At times like these, it's important to remember who's in the boat with you.

As a believer, we have to trust His character. If we believe that Jesus has all things in His control, then He will only allow trials to come that are for our good. In the story above, Jesus told the disciples to go to the other side. Jesus knew that no matter what was going to happen, He could handle it. And then He left the disciples alone—by going to sleep in the same boat—to allow the disciples to test, and therefore stretch, their faith.

Most trials come up to us without warning. Jesus didn't tell the disciples before He went to lie down in the bottom of the boat, "Hey guys, there's a storm coming. No matter how bad the storm gets, don't worry about it. We'll be fine. Just trust me." He didn't warn them. He let the trial blindside them.

And they reacted like most of us would. They questioned Jesus' character. They wondered if Jesus cared. Did He know that they were going to die? Was Jesus paying any attention at all? And if He knew, why didn't He warn them? Why wasn't He doing anything about it? They suddenly found it hard to believe that Jesus was who He said He was.

It's normal human nature to expect smooth sailing once you become a believer. But Jesus told us to prepare for war, not peace (Matthew 10:34), to be wise and strategic (Matthew 10:16), and that unless your righteousness surpasses the Pharisees and teachers of the law, you won't get into Heaven (Matthew 5:20). That doesn't sound much like an easy going, easy ride kind of religion. In fact, Jesus said in John 16:33, *"In the world you will have tribulation; but be of good cheer, I have overcome the world."*

Jesus did tell us that the storm was coming. But He's in our boat, and He's already overcome the world. He calls us to be overcomers, too. *Who is he who overcomes the world, but he who believes that Jesus is the Son of God? (1John 5:5)* So that by belief in the One who overcomes, we also overcome the world. Christianity is a hard religion, if it was easy, G. K. Chesterton would never have said, "The Christian ideal has not been tried and found wanting; it has been found difficult and left untried." Most people come to the very cusp of Christianity, find out that it is not just worship songs and fellowship moments, and turn around and go back. Believers are not the spoiled brats of humanity—we don't always get what we want, and we, too, have to go through hard times. But the difference is that we have Jesus in our boat through every storm.

So what do we do when the storm comes? How does God want us to respond?

First, we have to stop wrestling with the trial. Imagine the disciples in the storm, battening down the hatches, bailing water out with buckets, trying to get everyone on the ship as safe as possible. They attempt to battle the storm alone. And fear gains the upper hand.

When we find ourselves in the midst of a trial, we may run around our ship with bailing buckets and tying down ropes, too. We may do everything we can think of to overcome this situation on our own, but sooner or later we discover that the storm is bigger and more powerful than we are alone. It's then we need to surrender – not to the trial or the storm, but to God. Stop fighting and seek out the lesson God wants you to learn. Remember, what you're going through right now is no surprise to Him. He knew this was coming and has allowed it into your life for a learning experience.

There is no fear in love; but perfect love casts out fear, because fear involves torment. But he who fears has not been made perfect in love. We love Him because He first loved us. (1 John 4:18-19)

Our love for God stems from His love for us. Each trial is an opportunity for us to learn that He loves us and to learn the full extent and direction of that love. He will not tempt us beyond what we can bear (1 Corinthians 10:13) and all things that happen in our lives happen for His purpose, and for our good. (Romans 8:28). If we trust these aspects of God's character, then we will have faith that He is in control, even when we are *not*. Provided that we remember the promises God has made to us in the midst of our trials, we can overcome our loss of control because we know the one who is in control.

DO YOU FEAR BEING ALONE?

When the disciples finally went down in the boat to get Jesus, they had held out as long as they could—too long actually—and had talked themselves into a frenzy of fear. "Teacher, do you not care that we are perishing?" They could have asked, "Do you care at all? Have you been paying attention? What are you doing? Where have you been?"

When we feel we're about to be capsized, feelings of helplessness and abandonment come crashing in like a tidal wave. When God doesn't come in and rescue us immediately, we feel abandoned by an insensitive God. Abandonment is a sore spot for many believers. Bad parenting, betrayals by friends, family, or even the church has made many of us feel the sting of insensitive people who we once trusted in our lives. But God does care. He is not insensitive and He has not abandoned us. No matter the trial, He is there, waiting for us to come to Him and ask for help.

"Be strong and of good courage, and do it; do not fear nor be dismayed, for the LORD God—my God—will be with you. He will not leave you nor forsake you, until you have finished all the work for the service of the house of the LORD." (1 Chronicles 28:20)

And He promises pretty much the same in:

- Deuteronomy 31:8

- Hebrews 13:5
  - Joshua 1:9
- Matthew 28:20.

If you have a moment, and need the blessing right now, go ahead and look up those verses in your Bible. Highlight them, write one on an index card to memorize and keep with you. This is important stuff. You are not alone, and God has promised to never leave you on your own. When you feel alone, it will be the perfect time to pull that index card out, read it, and pray on that promise.

Prayer is the ultimate expression of our need. Jesus does not smother us or push Himself on us. Sometimes He will hold back the comfort of His love simply because we haven't yet asked for it. We have a choice in this matter, and He wants us to choose Him. He wants us to depend on Him and no one else for that level of comfort. When we rely upon Him, He can fill our cup to overflowing.

DO YOU FEEL HELPLESS?

Often we try everything we can before we turn to God. But just like the disciples in the storm, our problem turns out much bigger than our capabilities. That's when God will wait until we realize that we are incapable of handling the situation ourselves. Sometimes it's only when we are powerless that we turn to God for help. When we finally do, we find that His promise to Paul in 1 Corinthians 12:9 is also meant for us: *And He said to me, "My grace is sufficient for you, for My strength is made perfect in weakness."* And when we find that this promise is a guarantee for us, too, we'll be able to open our hearts like Paul did and declare, *"Therefore most gladly I will rather boast in my infirmities, that the power of Christ may rest upon me."*

Our infirmities and our weakness have a purpose. They are not senseless acts of cruelty. The power of Christ rests upon us in the midst of our helplessness so that we become "one who is helped." All we have to do is ask the one who has the power to help. Prayer connects us immediately to the source of power, Jesus.

Do you think that the disciples' faith was greater before or after the storm? Once Jesus displayed His power over the storm, the disciples forgot about their near death experience immediately. They took their fearful eyes off the storm, and turned them on Jesus with awe and even more respect. The power that He showed to the disciples proved to them that He is able to deliver on His promises.

When you turn to Jesus, and He shows His power over the storm in your life, will your faith be greater before or after the trial? His power when you are helpless to do anything about your circumstances will make you boast about your infirmities. And that's exactly what Jesus wants from you—a witness with a testimony that will move others to believe. You can't have a testimony until you can tell others about how Jesus saved you, and He can't save you until you have gone through the storm.

Storms are coming, and we have to know how to respond to them. By going through them with Jesus, we will learn to be more like Him in the face of the next one. Jesus never feared, even though He was at all points tempted. He was without sin, even though He hungered, thirsted, was tired, and became angry. Through the gospels, we find that His trials proved His humanity. But unlike us, Jesus did not fear. It was because Jesus held strong to His faith. Faith is the opposite of fear. Jesus gave us the perfect example of what we are to strive for in this world: a sinless life that is in tune with God at all times, and lived without fear in spite of the trials. But in this fallen world, it's impossible for us to become sinless or fearless.

But Jesus beheld them, and said unto them, "With men this is impossible; but with God all things are possible." (Matthew 19:26 KJV)

Be assured that it is God's will that we live with peace in our hearts. By trusting God and His promises, the impossible becomes possible. We just have to learn to be more like Jesus and faithfully turn to Him when trials come and when fear rises. He is the one who can crush fear's head like a serpent under His heel. It is my prayer for you today that you will remember Him when you feel alone and that you will come to Him in prayer when you feel powerless and out of control.

For more, look for FREEDOM FROM FEAR

Available at your favorite book retailer.

About the Author

In simple language, Pauline Creeden breaks down Biblical stories and applies them to real life in new ways. Her methods of teaching have brought new light to old scriptures. Pauline is a horse trainer from Virginia, but writing is her therapy.

Connect with the author: http://fatfreefaith.com

Date

In Happy Times
PRAISE GOD
In Hard Times
SEEK GOD
In Quiet Times
WORSHIP GOD
In Painful Times
TRUST GOD
At All Times
THANK GOD

Date

In Happy Times
PRAISE GOD
In Hard Times
SEEK GOD
In Quiet Times
WORSHIP GOD
In Painful Times
TRUST GOD
At All Times
THANK GOD

Date

In Happy Times
PRAISE GOD
In Hard Times
SEEK GOD
In Quiet Times
WORSHIP GOD
In Painful Times
TRUST GOD
At All Times
THANK GOD

Date

In Happy Times
PRAISE GOD
In Hard Times
SEEK GOD
In Quiet Times
WORSHIP GOD
In Painful Times
TRUST GOD
At All Times
THANK GOD

Date

In Happy Times
PRAISE GOD
In Hard Times
SEEK GOD
In Quiet Times
WORSHIP GOD
In Painful Times
TRUST GOD
At All Times
THANK GOD

Date

In Happy Times
PRAISE GOD
In Hard Times
SEEK GOD
In Quiet Times
WORSHIP GOD
In Painful Times
TRUST GOD
At All Times
THANK GOD

Date

In Happy Times
PRAISE GOD
In Hard Times
SEEK GOD
In Quiet Times
WORSHIP GOD
In Painful Times
TRUST GOD
At All Times
THANK GOD

Date

In Happy Times
PRAISE GOD
In Hard Times
SEEK GOD
In Quiet Times
WORSHIP GOD
In Painful Times
TRUST GOD
At All Times
THANK GOD

Date

In Happy Times
PRAISE GOD
In Hard Times
SEEK GOD
In Quiet Times
WORSHIP GOD
In Painful Times
TRUST GOD
At All Times
THANK GOD

Date

In Happy Times
PRAISE GOD
In Hard Times
SEEK GOD
In Quiet Times
WORSHIP GOD
In Painful Times
TRUST GOD
At All Times
THANK GOD

Date

In Happy Times
PRAISE GOD
In Hard Times
SEEK GOD
In Quiet Times
WORSHIP GOD
In Painful Times
TRUST GOD
At All Times
THANK GOD

Date

In Happy Times
PRAISE GOD
In Hard Times
SEEK GOD
In Quiet Times
WORSHIP GOD
In Painful Times
TRUST GOD
At All Times
THANK GOD

Date

In Happy Times
PRAISE GOD
In Hard Times
SEEK GOD
In Quiet Times
WORSHIP GOD
In Painful Times
TRUST GOD
At All Times
THANK GOD

Date

In Happy Times
PRAISE GOD
In Hard Times
SEEK GOD
In Quiet Times
WORSHIP GOD
In Painful Times
TRUST GOD
At All Times
THANK GOD

50490247R00066

Made in the USA
Middletown, DE
25 June 2019